Ode to Journey of my Life

Kirandeep kaur

First Published in June 2022

ISBN: 978-93-5628-068-7

BLUEROSE PUBLISHERS
www.BlueRoseONE.com
info@bluerosepublishers.com
+91 8882 898 898

Cover Design:
Geetika Kandari

Typographic Design:
Sachvesh Srivastava

Distributed by: BlueRose, Amazon, Flipkart

Table of Contents

"A Beautiful Day"

Wasn't it a beautiful day? With the sky so blue and the birds that flew with their wings Spread out in search of food.

Wasn't it a beautiful day? with the sky so clear and bright and not a single speck of Cloud to be in sight. The Sun throwing Out its light to make the day more bright.

Wasn't it a beautiful day? with the sun so bright and hot, The flowers and trees dancing in their place to and fro. And the Nature playing its part with happy look in heart.

Book's

Books are my passion when I read one it gives me various lessons.

Books, Books, Books? Please do take a look. At these thin and thick Books. Precious Books for books are a source of Joy like a adventurous boy.

If a Child needs to learn skill, he can take a book to grill.

If a hungry man wants to cook he can take a recipe book and Cook.

Book are great fun like a rising Sun. Books in the library seem like a Valley full of variety of flowers.

Books are my friend with them I can live an never ending trend.

"Bouncing Back"

He Said I love you but he really didn't Care He always
talked about feelings which were really aren't there.

I never knew your heart Could break my and all the
vows that were our part.

He held my hand to make me believe he was forever
mine but actually be was lying. Now, I know he used me
I thought he was my life but he was a secret knife.

If I'd never met you, I wouldn't have never felt the pain,
Yes! the pain, this pain making me insane.
Thank god I have power to bend down otherwise this
pain would make me drain.

I will get up again, move forward never to look back
and brighten up my days with right track.

Broken Me

The World that surrounds me is broken up and broken is me. To mend it or set it right is not every ones Cup of tea.

Broken are relations and Broken nations. Broken are husband and Wives, broken that cannot be mended are their lives.

My Broken heart that really hurts. Broken churches that end up searches.

Broken shores locking Success doors. Broken is my love that kills my inside dove.

Broken world and people Can never be mended. Such
Everlasting quarrels, I fear if can it ever be repaired.

Broken love that kills the beautiful dove.

Broken world, and people can never be mended.

Such ever lasting quarrels, I fear if Can ever be ended.

"Broken Promises"

Written By Kirandeep in the year 1997 Place of writing Mussoorie

Many Promises were made Many Commitments were made

Many order have been bade

But, were they kept?

Or all just swept, with swing of time. Lost were the stars of shine. God promised a wonderful Universe

Mankind promised a faithful earth Leaders promised strong nations. I kept patience and Waited.

But none were kept
Yes none were kept.
Truly said, wisely said all promises were
Crushed flew in dust

" I Can Till feel his Touch"

No Words Can define his touch It's hard for Me to forget his touch, an unexplainable feeling which makes everything refresh.

His passionate eyes, his hands tough but with such affection he kisses, it makes me mad and crazy further more.

When he holds me close heart pumps so strong the blood in the vein runs like never ending rain.

We share a very minimal time but his hands touching like something divine.

His hot breath, his skin touching my skin it feels as every thing is just win win.

His eyes breaking through my soul, he gives me what I always longed for.

Every time he touches me it feels the first time. I would do anything for that touch, that feel, that closeness, with him my world sublime.

Clouds

Like fluffs of cotton spotless white,

I wandered places far and wide.

Over gales, hills and valleyed tops, thy I floated and dance on Himalayan drops.

Water from the air and trees, fills my belly with the breeze. Turning to a darkish grey, I block the sun light's yellow rays.

A thunderstrom of light, fills the mortals with delight. And It begins to crackle and rain, to water little fields of grain.

Hungry again I float away, making room for sunshine way. Soon I will return again, to water little fields of grain.

Come, My Little Girl

Come, my little girl, here are chocolates for you; some chocolate are waffey some are with gems and some of new trends.

My little girl chocolates are good to eat and they are sweet, I know you like it when you need a good treat. My girl learn to share the chocolates I get for her, although I know you like them after a good rest.

Daughter

Oh! Baby your love
Is like sunshine
Turning my pain into
Happiness, your little
Soul enlightens my goal.

Beheld in your lighted
Spirit, I see myself
As amirate.

You are a shining
Stream and your love is a beautiful
Dream.

Your image in my
Mind is so clean
“Jagvi” you are
My baby queen

Examination

Oh, dear examination,
I have made no
Preparation I am
Afraid of you
Kindly tell me what to do.
Exam, Exams, Exams,
They come every year,
We must pull up our gears.
Study, revise and learn
Parents, teachers
Makes us groan
You come always early, but I am late, you
Love me but I hate
I must admit I hate exams
As there is too much cram , cram and cram.

"Good Day"

It's a good day
It's a good day
The day when everything
Is in a good way.
I went to office
Everything was good
I came home, it was all good. I ate my
Food it was good.
I whisper and shout
Still it was good.

I watched television
Everything played was good
Good was my friend
And good were the word I penned.

Goodness and Greatness

Goodness is the only investment that never fails, it is a famous saying which prevails. It is nice to be great but it is better trying to be good and to be great.

Goodness is a quality of heart where as greatness is a quality of mind. Goodness comes with in and greatness with time.

A stateman thinks of next generation while politician thinks of election.

Prophets like Buddha, Mahavira, Jesus, Mohammad and Gandhi professed goodness and with the process they were the greatest.

Endeavour in life to be good and then great blended with harmony it will grace.

Happy feast

If you want to
Feed the guest
And few to impressed
Then start with something hot and spicy and anything best and dicey
Guest like all types of food, chicken curry, pranthas with pick limes, and soup heated many times.

Follow my recipe of sauce, potato, curd and garlic with green chilli on Desi paranthas and serve it with grace like a boss.

If you ever fall in love

If you ever fall in love fall in love with some one who wants to know your favourites and finest traits.

If you ever fall in love, fall in love with someone who love to see you smile and showers love as long as river mile.

If you ever fall in love fall in love with someone who gets calm in your arms.

If you ever fall in love fall in love with someone who is proud to be with you in public, kisses you, cuddles you shows you, owes you like a couplet.

If you ever fall in love fall in love with someone who will never abuse, use you and misuse.

Its My Life

Its my life,
Its now or never
Life is unique in
Its own style
And everyone has
Their on strife.
Listen to the positive
The voice that talks
You down, it shouldn't
Be around.
We live only once
Do what you feel like, live the way you want too, none will cry with you in your pain, just refrain from the vain.

Yes!

I am going to live for even its my life, its now or never, its now or never.

Life and cricket

Life is a game of cricket
With a fear of losing a wicket
If you have to bowl
Do not start to howl
If you are selected
To bat, accept it with
A wave of your hat
If you are caught
Or bowled for a naught
Then do not cry
Nor ask for why?
Just think and you
Will know in a while
Here someone wins,
Other losses a wicket

My country my pride

India my Country
Where veda and upnishid
Flow
Blessed with greenery
India my country

India my country
I love to be part of the rich heritage
Betowed with rich culture. India, my
Maternal land.
Here great worriers
Are born, and goddess and the domain
It's the land of
Sages and its existence
Is from ages.

We should be united to create a better domain. This is India, where transparency is a new game.

I love my country its my pride and it gives me confidence to move with stride.

My Goal

No matters what may come
I will reach my goal
For my life's goal like all
Others is a piece of land to dig a grave, where I shall lie peacefully with a tree bent over to give me shock. Some flowers growing close by me.

Will decorate my grave and symbolize life.
Visitor would come to mourn and some will cherish my memory still fresh in their minds. I would love if the people I love today, come and sit by my grave tomorrow to make my soul not feel sorrow.

Night

Every dark night casting
Its spell upon us,
And we being ignored out of the fact die each night.

No wonder, thinking on of it , I am positive sooner do
I realise with night passes our life.
After tiring day, we crave for a peaceful night although
we know we loose most part our life in bed, but never
do we realize the fact so said.

Yet, do not mourn every dark night wakes up to bright
dawn.

Our Puppy : Tuffy

We bought a puppy and named it tuffy.
It was a white pomerian
Tiny little and fluffy.

It was a cute little
Little toy for my daughter's
Joy, playing with it was
Her only hoy.

We loved it dearly but it stayed with us bearly.

Tuffy was with us for, a year, for we adopted it to a
family to save it from tears.

"Failure"

Written by Kirandeep Kaur in year 1998 place of writing Mussoorie

I tried to smile, but these were silent tears in my eyes.

I tried to dream, but Fantasy was out of my access.
I tried to speak, but silence sealed my sighs.

I tried to be successfully but failures stopped my sighs.

I tried to be successful but failures stopped my ways,
But I used failures a manure, and watered the plant of hope,
Then outgrew the tree of progress.

"A Tribute to Lata Ji"

Written By Kirandeep Kaur Year 2022 at Panchkula.

The fairest Melody queen of all was Lata ji,
She was rhythm of every heart from India to Indiana.

A unique person in everyway with her own class and style her voice would brighten anybody as would her charming smile.

A perfect singer for her audiences, she showered them with more than 30,000 songs. Her singing talent and voice modulation was as great as her simple and pious personality.

Lata Ji queen of people's heart : that's what she wanted to be from an early age, she played the part of a symbol of selfless humanity and also a patriot.

Emitting from vina of saraswati due to vibration of strings, the voice of Lata ji is certainly like the perpetual stream.

Her death touched off an avalanche of grief, all around the world. As the news of her death spread people sang her songs with gloomy heart and head.

As was befitting her life, which had drawn to a close, her funeral was one dignity and beauty.

She was termed as "nightangle" for on her death, as in her, life, she makes our hearts with caring touch, this queen of melody who gave us so much.

Poetry to me

Poetry to me is music, an expression of heart, I can feel it in my veins, as a thought starts and words like music flow, I pen them down like rain.

I can feel the words flowing, my mind are clean and serene. It's lovely when I see the words making rhythm like easy algorithm.

A fresh poetry is like a untouch dew, it flows in my blood like something new. My words speak my heart poetry to me is an art.

Rejection

I too have known rejection, I too have known what it is to feel rejected, not accepted and suddenly not all looks great.

Oh! That corner in my room, your comfort is great, your space is never a trait, rather in my room I narrate. That corner in my room never troll and their I feel i am in my own role.

It has saved my life, that corner in my room, my study table, the papers my pen and the emotions of words begun.

"Search For A Friend"

A question absurb : friend is the word myth or real?

To me a friend is one who cares and makes the world seem fresh and new, who understands your point of view and let you remain you.

As she sighs warm breath she takes me to the point of death she is a person like you and does things, which you like to do.

That carefree smile, that intense look that makes you long for her by hook or crook.

Who comes closes to the idea of the person you.

Would like to grow with who makes you believe that he is real and not just a myth.

"Spirit Of Love"

Written By Kirandeep Kaur in the Year 1999 place of writing (Mussoorie)

As I gazed at the stars strewn in the heaven above a great ecstasy possessed me and it rose again the spirit of love. Soon it grew restless in me as I looked for down the shimmering sea.

I walked out of my cottage on that warm summer night filled with the bliss of solitude into that blessed lover of moon light. My heart was light and I felt as though, I had drifled with the wind, blowing so low.

Dawn crept on ...... slowly and steadily then I saw the first rays of the morning sun as though emerging from the sea that flowed so gently.

I sat there on the castle ruins and noticed not the creeping hours of time. I had not thought it was a Sunday.

Until I heard the bells of the church chime. And then towards the church, I ran down the path that was over flowing with life's wet happiness and joy and then I knew that the spirit of love had bound me to all these natural things...

Summer

The street cars
Are like hot case
All basking in
Sun rays.

The Sunshines
Bright the street
No sooner does it
Ignite with hot treat.

And every where the
People go....

With a sun glow.

The Aeroplane

How do you like to go up in the sky?
Up in the sky so blue and high
The aeroplane can take you up through the
Clouds, sailing in the blue sky, Oh the pleasantest
Thing a child can fly.

Up in the sky over the buildings, which I can see twinkling river and trees and mountains all seemed like a winking up in the air I go flying. A dream so true in the aeroplane flying and flying

Walk with my pet

I like to walk with my pet
his steps are short
Like mine, but his runs is not divine
He doesn't say, hurry up he doesn't talk at all he is so cute that we almost play and fall.

I see people in hurry, they don't stop and see
But I am glad I walk with my pet who is fun loving.

www.ingramcontent.com/pod-product-compliance
Ingram Content Group UK Ltd.
Pitfield, Milton Keynes, MK11 3LW, UK
UKHW040014200726
13854UKWH00001B/190

9 789356 280687